Powerful People Are Powerful Leaders

A  Book

Powerful People
Are
Powerful Leaders

Your Daily Guide
to Becoming a Powerful Leader

A "Power Series" Book

Peter Biadasz and Richard Possett

A  Book

iUniverse, Inc.
New York Lincoln Shanghai

Powerful People Are Powerful Leaders
Your Daily Guide to Becoming a Powerful Leader

iUniverse books may be ordered through booksellers or by contacting:

iUniverse
2021 Pine Lake Road, Suite 100
Lincoln, NE 68512
www.iuniverse.com
1-800-Authors (1-800-288-4677)

ISBN-13: 978-0-595-41218-1 (pbk)
ISBN-13: 978-0-595-85576-6 (ebk)
ISBN-10: 0-595-41218-1 (pbk)
ISBN-10: 0-595-85576-8 (ebk)

Printed in the United States of America

lead·er·ship

NOUN:

1. The position or office of a leader: *ascended to the leadership of the party.*
2. Capacity or ability to lead: *showed strong leadership during her first term in office.*
3. A group of leaders: *met with the leadership of the nation's top unions.*
4. Guidance; direction: *The business prospered under the leadership of the new president.*

❦ ❧

lead·er   (lē′dər) KEY

NOUN:

1. One that leads or guides.
2. One who is in charge or in command of others.
3. One who has influence or power.

Dedications

I dedicate this book to the memory of Paul Gray, a man who clearly demonstrated all the leadership qualities discussed in this book.

~ Peter Biadasz

This book is dedicated to the natural leaders in each and every one of us. For it is our duty to search-out those hidden qualities within us and nurture them to the full benefit of mankind.

~ Richard Possett

Acknowledgements

I can't say this enough—thank you to my family, my friends and my business associates; you add so much to my personal and professional life. Even though I may not always show it, know that my appreciation runs very deep.

~ Peter Biadasz

Kudos is the order of the day for Norman J.E. Roe. He is the one person in my life who manifested the true qualities of a quintessential leader. Norm always set the best example of leadership by leading people with the good example.

~ Richard Possett

Why Read This Book?

As the world turns, we all have choices. In both our personal and professional lives we may choose to lead, follow, or kindly get out of the way. Humanity would be much better served if everyone decided to be their best; to use their God given talents to the maximum. Unfortunately, this is not what happens in the real world. Therefore, with our own free will, we decide. Each day of the week, and month of the year, we select our words, behaviors, and actions from the smorgasbord of life. We have a myriad of alternatives available to us. It is our choice to choose. We can either exercise it rightly, or abdicate it, conscientiously or unconscientiously.

In the course of human events, it is critical to have moral leaders. We need the noble chieftains who will step forward and guide the masses to where they may not want to go. It's simply the way it is and the leaders are the ones that point the way. These good men and women are going somewhere and they have the power to persuade other people to go with them. Leaders have thoughtful objectives and strategies. They have the knowledge and the personal will to execute upon those elements.

Dale McConkey is often quoted as saying… "The leader understands that sustained long-term results cannot be achieved by pushing people to do things. He attracts followers in much the same way as a magnet attracts particles of metal." As you can see, the true commander has the magnetism and power to take people to a place where they would not have gone by themselves.

Do you want to be a more powerful person—powerful at home, work, and play? Of course, your answer is a powerful YES! But, real power is not physical strength. Real power is the knack of getting along; having people respect you and working with others for bilateral benefit. It's the capacity to make friends, create relationships, and influence people. Real power is having an extensive *circle of influence* enabling you to get things done right—right now. It's the ability to motive others for *win-win* situations and mutual advantage. It is having the capability to lead.

Through effective and ethical leadership we become a powerful person. For with responsibility, that is properly executed, comes power and success. Thus, **Powerful People Are Powerful Leaders** ~ Your Daily Guide To Becoming A Powerful Leader is the book for you if you choose to be a captain among men. If you wish to add the strength and energy of leadership to your associations with family, friends, and fellow travelers, then buy, read, and study this book.

Having power in a leadership role may denote, to some, holding control or domination over another. This is false assumption. In the context of this book, power is used to mean the vim, vigor, vitality, and virtue in your personal involvement with individuals and groups. It is not autocratic and dictatorial command. Said differently, it is the soundness, strength, and stalwartness of your personality that provides the continued benevolent sovereignty over people. It is something given and not taken. Therefore, to create and maintain a power-driven leadership position means to have all of your associations with your fellow-man be masterful, pervasive, and powerful.

Power is that essential energy, intensity, and well-being that you contribute to the leadership process. It is what makes leading people truly valuable, full of meaning, and gives it longevity. Ones forceful-energy working with people for a greater good produces an agreeable effect upon the personal mind, body, and spirit, as well as that of the entire community. It makes our worldly attachments more pleasing, positive, and productive. It is this healthy fulfillment in our role as a captain among men that is rewarding and rich. Thus, these are the reasons why power-driven people become powerful leaders.

They say leaders are born. Well, who are they? An ultimate leader may first come into the world with a propensity to lead. But, effective and mature leadership is truly developed. It is realized through both nature and nurture. This is so because the qualities and characteristics needed to manifest and nourish the leader skills were generally not taught to us very well as we were growing up. This faculty is typically a learned behavior in life through observation and, most often, experienced by trial and error.

Throughout life we develop habits for leading others. Sometimes we develop certain practices that are useful, such as good communications capabilities; and, at other times we develop counterproductive behaviors, such as having to always be right. New leadership patterns can be learned and old hurtful actions and attitudes modified. In that endeavor, behavior changes slowly. However, with simple day-by-day reminders, as well as diligent practice and application, new-found leader capabilities can easily be imbedded into your everyday world and culture.

Right now you are reading a one-of-a-kind book. There is nothing else like it on the bookshelf. The text is unique because of its multidimensional nature. The manuscript focuses on leadership at home, work, and play in both personal and professional situations. The book is a practical, inspirational, and educational guide on developing the skills needed to form more pleasant and productive leadership roles. Although the book is comprehensively compelling, it is still simple and easy.

By design, this book is simple to read and the assignments are easy to complete. This format allows you to learn new leadership proficiency each and every day and encourages you to practice and apply your new found knowledge. It gives you a fresh awareness of the way you relate to others and suggestions for positive change. For you see, this book is a once a day, fast and easy, excursion into having greater dynamic leadership competence and therefore, being a more powerful person.

This book is not intended to be an elixir, i.e. to solve all of your leadership inquires and issues. Many factors come into play in building the requisite qualities in leaders and this book does not address all of them. The intention of this book is to help you become aware, in a general sense, of the ways you are currently relating to others and then, to become mindful that there may be other ways, better methods and modes, to conduct yourself.

Read this book; do the exercises every day and apply what you are learning to your leadership circumstances. By the time you are finished, you should be a more knowledgeable person with new confidence in your personal and professional leadership capabilities. As you progress through this book, you will discover both your good leadership patterns and your poor ones. You will grow more confident each day by building on your strengths and reducing your limitations.

Each day you will learn an inspirational quote. The quotes were chosen for their content and message rather than the origin of the quote. Be that as it may, fact-find the authors. In doing so you may just become an enhanced and well-rounded individual. It can be highly interesting to learn about the quote source and why, when, and where the author may have expressed it. With your research and education about these powerful people you emerge as a real renaissance person. Being able to discuss intelligently with others what you have learned will help you to be more conversant, interesting, and sought after resource. This ability will help you feel more at ease in associations with others. It will help make you a more effective leader as a power-driven individual.

By completing the daily lessons, you become increasingly knowledgeable and educated about leadership and powerful leaders. Give thoughtful consideration to the lessons and what you gain by doing them thoroughly. Finishing the tasks alone, however, will not yield a successful result unless you actually apply what you have learned. Just making a list or writing down your thoughts will not be of complete assistance unless you integrate that knowledge into your everyday behavior. It is one thing to know what to do and yet still another to truly do it. Work on it and make it work in your personal environment and professional surroundings. If you are diligent in your work, it works.

A real unique bonus in this book is that you can reflect upon all your efforts after six months. This process gives you an honest chance to fully reevaluate your new skills and discover if what you are doing is working productively for you. By learning the daily lessons and applying one exercise each day into your business and personal world, you will become more learned and confident in your leadership situations. And, as you sow, you shall reap wonderful individual benefits.

In the practical world, it is the still-silence and bright-glow of power that makes for a leader. But what comes first, power or leadership? There is no doubt in the views of the authors that to be truly powerful, you must first be accepted as a leader. Possessing the qualities and characteristics of leadership will help you to be more efficient and effective in your daily life. Competence and efficaciousness begets followship. And, the more people who are willing to follow you, the more you can get things done. Thus, much of your success in leadership is about being productive. It's about immediate results. It's about be followed by others. It's about the ability to command. This book will help you become a power-driven person by improving your capabilities to lead people.

Table of Contents

Preface

The truly talented, a rare few, may have been born true leaders. To the vast majority of us, leadership is an acquired life skill. To highly varying degrees we all learn about leadership at home, in church, on the playground, in the classroom, at college, in the workplace, and from all of our other everyday life experiences. But, be certain that for the most of us, it is an acquired skill that needs continued and ongoing attention. In the pages that follow, you are given an opportunity, in a fast and easy way, to develop your leadership abilities in a simple and fun method.

Let there be no doubt that this book is about leadership. That is, the guidance of a leader. Some people might rephrase the aforementioned definition to say—the position of a person that leads. But for us, this is a misleading statement of the term. You see, an individual manifests true leadership through direction, persuasion, tutelage, example, and charisma. A genuine leader doesn't gain their position of leadership through agency authority. People lead from power; the force of guidance, influence, teaching, and precedent. Power also includes that very special quality which captures the imagination and inspires loyalty. Therefore, our meaning of leadership is powerful because a real leader will develop and exercise these power skills. They will use their ability to guide people to a predetermined goal or objective. Their way is not a selfish and/or parochial protocol. For the true leader will guide with mutual respect and for bilateral benefit.

In this text we speak to the power skills of guidance, sway, personality, teaching, and example. The book is composed of daily assignments about leaders and leadership. These lessons are laid-out in four sections.

The first part of a daily drill is an inspiring quotation from a powerful person. The idea here is to thoughtfully reflect upon the passage as it relates to the subject matter. This simple daily practice may help coalesce the leader concepts and principles into your personal minds-eye.

Next, the work guide asks you, the reader, to do research on the quotation. This task can easily take you back in time and into the circumstances involving the words spoken by the author of the quote. This process can help you to understand your forebears and their historical significance. We are told that those who forget history are destined to relive it. Your new applied knowledge can help you to avoid that potential mistake. Furthermore, having this store of learning makes you somewhat of a renaissance person. This faculty should cause you to be a more interesting and sought after individual. Having this talent is a great contributor to good interpersonal skills.

The third segment of our daily assignment is a straightforward set of exercises. They should be thoroughly completed. Typically, this task is in an easy question and answer format. For you see, this book is not a comprehensive study of leaders and their leadership ability. Clearly, that would require a complete course on leader scholarship. This book is constructed upon a set of fast and easy tasks for everyday practical utility. It is designed to slowly and carefully help you become more powerful in your leader situations. The daily assignments are simple and straightforward drills. Each one is a small building block of knowledge. We liken them to the brick and mortar constructing a school of powerful leadership in your whole being. Your foundation for leadership is developed brick by brick; one scoop of mortar at a time.

Finally, the last part of the work is a six months review. This activity provides the occasion to reexamine and reevaluate your preexisting completed and assigned lessons. This practice reinforces your book of knowledge on leaders and leadership. Behavior can be learned and modified easier through review and repetition. Thus, our process helps you to reinforce and strengthen your knowledge and therefore, become a more power-driven person, one day at a time.

The principles in this book have been realized from two long and productive business careers. We walk the walk. We practice what we preach. We are confident that the quotations in this book will inspire you to do the same. As completed, the daily lessons will make you a more dynamic leader. The completed work should take you beyond mediocrity in business and at home. Please carefully read, and then rigorously fill in the blanks for more knowledge in your life. We pray that you have a great day and a better tomorrow as you work your way to greater leadership success.

~ Peter Biadasz and Richard Possett

(Before proceeding, consider turning to page 211 and read more about the authors. Their life history, work experiences, and expertise may give you a better frame of reference, insights, and perspective regarding the contents of this book.)

Foreword

By
Vicki Anderson
Leadership Consultant
Anderson Resources

This book may change your life. Only you will be able to know for sure. My father always said, "Anything worth doing is worth doing well." If you wish to become a more powerful leader, you must invest in yourself and define your own philosophy about people. Your philosophy about people and relationships will have a great impact on your leadership style.

There are many books about leadership trying to tell you what you should do and how you should act. Few books give you the opportunity to reflect on that advice and decide how to put it into practice for yourself. This book does just that. In bite-sized pieces each day, you will be asked to read and reflect, study and internalize, or affirm and validate what you think leadership is all about.

The simple is often the most profound. Anyone who has ever accomplished anything worth having will tell you that it is consistency and persistence that pays off more than great ideas and lots of money. With your consistency and persistence through the simple processes of this book, you will gain insights and confidence in the way you lead.

Being powerful does not mean having more authority; it means having the knowledge and confidence to know when and how to act for the best outcome. As you move along your journey during the next year, you may not be able to tell the difference daily, but by the time you are in your second six months and reviewing the earlier activities, you will begin to see your power grow.

I commend you on your choice to embark on this journey. This book will be a useful tool in your development. You may even find yourself using some of the quotes with others. After all, the best way to learn is to teach others what you have studied. May your learning help you become a powerful leader worth following.

Introduction

What Is Leadership?

"There are times to lead and there are times to follow. Knowing the difference is the way of the true leader." There are a myriad of definitions of leadership. To find one, start with the dictionary or simply visit your local public library. The bookstores have hundreds upon hundreds of literary works concerning leaders and leadership on their shelves. They can be viewed while you enjoy a hot cup of coffee. The subject can be researched on the Internet by viewing page after page of information. In this vast collection of knowledge you will not find a better description of the term than that written above.

As you attempt to define, in your own terms, the meaning of leadership, know that the most important person you will ever lead…is YOU!

What (Or Who) Is A Powerful Person?

A powerful person is someone who gets things done when they need to be done. They do it! They do it right! And, they do it right now! Power-driven people are the class president, team captain, chief executive, military commander, and community leader. Truthfully, they typically are the nerds of the world. So be careful what you do on the playground and on your way up the corporate hierarchy. These types of individuals always seem to have time for improved performance at work, home, and play. They eat right and exercise. They take time out in their day for reading, whether it is personal or professional. Power people pay attention to themselves and their relationships with other folks. They generally oversee people, but most importantly they manage themselves really well. Powerfully performing individuals control their time, actions, and results. They are self-reliant. Power performers take charge and responsibility. They don't play the blame game. They are self-confident, but not cocky. They are highly self-disciplined. They are self-motivated. When called upon to do the job, they get results on time. They do this in both their personal and professional worlds. They always perform powerfully. Power people have created a personal culture, a way of living life, of performing at the highest level.

How To Use This Book

This manuscript is styled as an interactive workbook on leadership. It contains simple and straightforward daily exercises. By no means is this book meant to be a comprehensive self-study course on how to interact with and lead people. The purpose of this workbook is to create a strong individual awareness in the readers mind about how they relate to and lead others. The intent of the writing is to inform the readers about common sense characteristics of leadership and associations between individuals and groups. It is not a new theory, but a time-tested practical guide to creating and sustaining powerful leadership roles. The objective of the exercises is to reinforce these basic principles. The quotations help validate the elements of what makes up the fun and functional leadership of our fellow human beings. Everyday you are given an opportunity to become more proficient in the skills necessary for powerful leadership. If you complete the daily tasks as asked, overtime you will incrementally amass a compendium of knowledge on leading people. If you then properly apply this learning in your daily life, the leadership situations with your family, friends, and fellow workers will become more powerful, one day at a time.

Six Months Review

This book is a one year odyssey about leadership. It is divided into two six month segments. The first section has to do with daily quotations and assignments helping to establish a consciousness of our leadership capabilities. The exercises help to identify counterproductive behavior patterns that should be corrected for more successful interactions with the people in our lives. The material also identifies new habits that might be established to strengthen the bonds between the people with which we associate. In the second six months, you have the opportunity to add depth, modify and reinforce what they had learned during the first part of the program. At the end of one year, you should have addressed the key result areas that will make your leadership abilities more powerful.

Sample Illustration

January 1
July 1

"Good followship comes from the sagacity to follow. Good leadership from the audacity to lead. And, the great leaders know the difference."

Vanposetski

Note the names of two leaders in the community that you know. Contact them for a meeting to discuss leadership. During the meeting, ask them for their particular meaning of leadership.

Name   *Thomas C. Sabin*

Action: *Telephone Tom to schedule a luncheon meeting and discuss his views on being a leader and his personal leadership skills.*

Name: *Mary H. Lamb*

Action: *Contact Mary at the next association dinner and set-up a meeting with her to explore leaders and leadership principles.*

Six Months Review:

We had lunch with Tom and he feels that leadership is the ability to skillfully influence people to take a special course of action with passion and a sense of urgency. We met with Mary and she believes that leadership is the silent ability to guide, direct and influence people to a meaningful end.

About The Quote Sources

If you desire to receive some further rewards from the daily exercises, do research on the people quoted on the pages in this book. You are encouraged to learn about their unique lives and special times. Learning how these individuals became power-driven people in their own right can be fascinating, if not educational. If someone happens to be quoted more than once, research the circumstances surrounding the quotation. In the instances of sayings and proverbs, a study into the traditions associated with each aphorism may be instructive. Consider doing the same for the unknown authors. Getting to know the composer of the quote and the particulars surrounding the passages can be a meaningful journey into history. The results of your study and research can be placed in the lines provided which are labeled as "Quotation Source Information." Here we have an important announcement: please understand that in instances in which a quote or manuscript text refers to "him" that the word "her" can simply be substituted

And please remember…

"The wisdom of the wise, and the experience of the ages,
may be preserved by quotation."
~ *Benjamin Disraeli*

And we say…

Tell me…I'll forget

Show me…I'll remember

Involve me…I'll comprehend

So, get involved to be great, to get better!

BE A POWERFUL LEADER!

January 1
July 2

"Where there is no vision the people perish."

Solomon

Effective and successful leadership is about leading according to the vision (plan/goal) about which you are passionate. What three key visions (plans/goals) do you have for you and your future?

_____

_____

_____

_____

_____

_____

Next to each write one thing that you will do before you go to bed tonight to take a step in realizing that vision for your life.

Six Months Review:

_____

_____

_____

Quotation Source Information:

_____

_____

_____

January 2
July 3

> "Leadership…is both something you are and something you do. But effective leadership starts with character."

Fred Smith

How you act or think when no one will know your actions or thoughts defines character. Who are people you consider leaders of high character?

1. _____

   _____

2. _____

   _____

3. _____

   _____

Contact each person listed today to find out the foundation upon which each has based his or her character.

Six Months Review:

_____
_____
_____

Quotation Source Information:

_____
_____
_____

January 3
July 4

"Integrity is the quality or state of being of sound moral principle; uprightness, honesty, and sincerity."

Webster's Dictionary

Integrity is an indispensable trait of a true leader. What other personality attributes do you believe make for a good leader? Why?

_____

_____

_____

_____

_____

Six Months Review:

_____

_____

_____

Quotation Source Information:

_____

_____

_____

January 4
July 5

"To grasp and hold a vision, that is the very essence of successful leadership—not only on the movie set where I learned it, but everywhere."

Ronald Reagan

What are the most important visions (goals) for your future in the personal side of your life?

1. _____
   _____

2. _____
   _____

3. _____
   _____

What are the main visions (goals) for your future professional life?

1. _____
   _____

2. _____
   _____

3. _____
   _____

Six Months Review:

_____

_____

_____

Quotation Source Information:

_____

_____

_____

January 5
July 6

"Lead by example."

Peter Biadasz

When there is consistency between what you say and your actions you earn respect. Who do you admire because they lead by example? Contact each to learn their perspective of leadership.

Name: _____

Perspective: _____

_____

Name: _____

Perspective: _____

_____

Name: _____

Perspective: _____

_____

Six Months Review:

_____

_____

_____

Quotation Source Information:

_____

_____

_____

January 6
July 7

"If you are ashamed to stand by your colors, you had better find another flag."

Afflatus

This I say to you: loyalty to your company; allegiance to your country; fealty to your family and faithfulness to yourself. Think about it. Write your thoughts down. Do you need to changes colors?

Company: _____

_____

Country: _____

_____

Family: _____

_____

Yourself: _____

_____

Other: _____

_____

Six Months Review:

_____
_____
_____

Quotation Source Information:

_____
_____
_____

January 7
July 8

"Speak when you are angry and you will make the best speech you will ever regret."

Ambrose Bierce

Angry words are regrettable. When was the last time you spoke in anger? Write down the situation. Consider apologizing to the person for speaking angry words.

_____

_____

_____

Six Months Review:

_____

_____

_____

Quotation Source Information:

_____

_____

_____

January 8
July 9

"Don't tell people how to do things, tell them what to do and let them surprise you with their results."

George S. Patton

List bosses or teachers that you had, who were masters at telling others what to do and letting them discover their own style in completing the task/assignment.

Name: _____

_____

Name: _____

_____

Name: _____

_____

List what made each of their styles unique to your learning experience.

Six Months Review:

_____

_____

_____

Quotation Source Information:

_____

_____

_____

January 9
July 10

"The ear of the leader must ring with the voices of the people."

Woodrow Wilson

Do you listen to the advice of the people you manage?　　　Yes/No

What specific tactics do you utilize to accomplish that feat?

_____
_____
_____
_____
_____

Six Months Review:

_____
_____
_____

Quotation Source Information:

_____
_____
_____

January 10
July 11

"Really big people are, above anything else, courteous, considerate and generous—not just too some people in some circumstances—but to everyone at all times."

Thomas J. Watson, Sr.

Choose three people: be courteous to one, considerate to the other, and generous to the last. Note how this activity made you feel as a person.

Name: _____

Courteous: _____

_____

Name: _____

Considerate: _____

_____

Name: _____

Generous: _____

_____

Six Months Review:

_____

_____

_____

Quotation Source Information:

_____

_____

_____

January 11
July 12

"Leadership is the art of getting someone else to do something you want done because he wants to do it."

Dwight Eisenhower

Have you ever been convinced to happily do something that you did not want to do? Who have you personally been around who that have been master motivators?

Name: _____

_____

Name: _____

_____

Name: _____

_____

What qualities made each person a master motivator?

Six Months Review:

_____

_____

_____

Quotation Source Information:

_____

_____

_____

January 12
July 13

"A leader is someone you choose to follow to a place you wouldn't go by yourself."

Joel Barker

Why would someone choose to follow another who had no idea where he was going or how he was going to get there, or even why he was going in the first place? List reasons why you have chosen to follow leaders in the past.

_____
_____
_____
_____
_____

List reasons why someone should follow your leadership.

1. _____
   _____

2. _____
   _____

3. _____
   _____

Six Months Review:

_____
_____
_____

Quotation Source Information:

_____
_____
_____

January 13
July 14

"I've learned that people will forget what you said, people will forget what you did, but people will never forget how you made them feel."

Maya Angelou

Some say charisma is an invisible energy with visible effects. What do you say? Who do you know that has charisma? How do they make you feel? Tell them!

Name: _____
_____

Name: _____
_____

Name: _____
_____

Six Months Review:
_____
_____
_____

Quotation Source Information:
_____
_____
_____

January 14
July 15

"The secret of getting ahead is getting started.
The secret to getting started is breaking your
complex overwhelming tasks into small manageable
tasks, and then starting on the first one."

Mark Twain

We have all been faced with a large, seemingly overwhelming task. What are some of the larger tasks you are or have been facing? Note each task and employ the Mark Twain approach. Note your progress.

Task: _____
_____

Task: _____
_____

Task: _____
_____

Six Months Review:
_____
_____
_____

Quotation Source Information:
_____
_____
_____

January 15
July 16

"The very essence of leadership is that you have to have vision. You can't blow an uncertain trumpet."

Theodore M. Hesburgh

Think about the greatest leaders you have followed. Have not all of them had a vision or plan of some sort they communicated to you? In what ways are you confident in the vision you have for your future and those around you?

1. _____
   _____

2. _____
   _____

3. _____
   _____

Six Months Review:

_____
_____
_____

Quotation Source Information:

_____
_____
_____

January 16
July 17

"Not being able to govern events, I govern myself."

Michel de Montaigne

Do you get wrapped-up in trying to govern events? If not, great! If so, make a list of the things you can do to redirect your efforts to be a better you. Then go out and do them.

1. _____
   _____

2. _____
   _____

3. _____
   _____

Six Months Review:
_____
_____
_____

Quotation Source Information:
_____
_____
_____

January 17
July 18

"There is nothing impossible to him who will try."

Alexander The Great

We all are told that certain accomplishments are impossible. Sometimes we are told to by others, sometimes it is told to us through negative self-talk. List things that you want to try that you have been told are impossible:

1. _____
   _____

2. _____
   _____

3. _____
   _____

Create an action plan to accomplish each task, including time lines.

Six Months Review:
_____
_____
_____

Quotation Source Information:
_____
_____
_____

January 18
July 19

"One of the best rules in life is, nothing is often a bad thing to do and always a clever thing to say."

Richard Possett

Recently, did you have a situation where you wished something went unsaid? Summarize it in the space below.

_____
_____
_____
_____
_____

Go back to the person and say it the right way or simply apologize.

Six Months Review:

_____
_____
_____

Quotation Source Information:

_____
_____
_____

January 19
July 20

"It is not in the still calm of life, or the repose of a pacific station, that characters are formed…Great necessities call out great virtues."

Abigail Adams

Consider the virtues of your character. What are they?

_____
_____
_____
_____
_____

How has necessity and adversity shaped them?

_____
_____
_____
_____
_____

Six Months Review:

_____
_____
_____

Quotation Source Information:

_____
_____
_____

January 20
July 21

When the character of a man is not clear to you, look at his friends.

Japanese Proverb

Most people like to associate with others that are similar to them. Who are some people you admire because of the friend's that they keep?

Name: _____
_____

Name: _____
_____

Name: _____
_____

Name: _____
_____

Name: _____
_____

What are the admirable attributes of each person?

Six Months Review:

_____
_____
_____

Quotation Source Information:

_____
_____
_____

January 21
July 22

"Leadership is action, not position."

Donald H. McGannon

We all know people who are leaders even though they may not be in a position of leadership. Theirs is a place of action, not an official title. Name people you respect as leaders because of the actions that they take:

Name: _____
_____

Name: _____
_____

Name: _____
_____

Call them today and let them know of your respect for them. Document highlights of the conversation.

Six Months Review:

_____
_____
_____

Quotation Source Information:

_____
_____
_____

January 22
July 23

"The next best thing to being clever is being able to quote someone who is."

Mary Pettibone Poole

Sometimes we can express ourselves better or even sound smarter and/or wiser than we really are by utilizing a well-timed quote. What are your favorite quotes?

1. _____
   _____

2. _____
   _____

3. _____
   _____

Six Months Review:

_____
_____
_____

Quotation Source Information:

_____
_____
_____

January 23
July 24

"One thing you can't recycle is wasted time."

Unknown

Whether we think we have mastered time management or can barely spell time management, we can always improve our skills in this vital area. List some of your biggest daily time wasters.

_____

_____

_____

_____

_____

Write down how you are going to immediately eliminate those time wasters from your life.

Six Months Review:

_____

_____

_____

January 24
July 25

"A good leader inspires others with confidence
in him; a great leader inspires them
with confidence in themselves."

Unknown

We all are more productive when we feel good about ourselves. In what
ways have leaders inspired confidence in you?

1. _____
   _____

2. _____
   _____

3. _____
   _____

4. _____
   _____

5. _____
   _____

Do the same for those that you lead.

Six Months Review:

_____
_____
_____

January 25
July 26

"A thick skin is a gift from God."

Konrad Adenauer

There is quite a bit of ambivalence in human nature related to leadership. Leaders are lied about, loved and hated at the same time, and simultaneously disparaged and praised. Truly, a good leader needs to be thick skinned. How about you? In the space below, note the many ways you could better shrug off personal criticism and be indifferent to insincere and unfair rumors and remarks.

_____

_____
_____
_____
_____

Six Months Review:

_____
_____
_____

Quotation Source Information:

_____
_____
_____

January 26
July 27

"The mediocre teacher tells. The good teacher
explains. The superior teacher demonstrates.
The great teacher inspires."

William Ward

Read the quote again substituting the word teacher with boss, leader, salesperson and parent.

List the people in each category who have inspired you the most:

Teacher: _____

Boss: _____

Leader: _____

Salesperson: _____

Parent: _____

How did each inspire you?

_____
_____
_____
_____
_____

Inspire others in your life following their examples.

Six Months Review:

_____

_____

_____

Quotation Source Information:

_____

_____

_____

January 27
July 28

"A man fails many times, but he is not a failure until he begins to blame somebody else."

John Burroughs

Taking responsibility is a key ingredient in leadership. List ways in which you can accept responsibility for your less than successful occurrences:

1. _____
   _____

2. _____
   _____

3. _____
   _____

Six Months Review:

_____
_____
_____

Quotation Source Information:

_____
_____
_____

January 28
July 29

> "'…but the Emperor has nothing on at all'
> cried the little child."

Hans Christian Anderson

Generally, children, drunkards, and fools tell the truth. They lack the mature mental capacity to separate fact from fiction. Analyze your truthfulness. Make a list of strengths and weaknesses.

Strengths:

_____

_____

Weaknesses:

_____

_____

Design a plan to strengthen your weaknesses.

_____

_____

_____

_____

Six Months Review:

_____

_____

_____

Quotation Source Information:

_____

_____

_____

January 29
July 30

"Success is not final, Failure is not fatal; it is the courage to continue that counts."

Winston Churchill

We usually do not know how much courage we posses until we are in difficult situations. Who are some of the most courageous people you know?

Name: _____
_____

Name: _____
_____

Name: _____
_____

Contact each and learn what makes each person courageous.

Six Months Review:

_____
_____
_____

Quotation Source Information:

_____
_____
_____

January 30
July 31

"If we all did the things we are capable of doing, we would literally astound ourselves."

Thomas Edison

We all have the ability to excel to be even greater than we currently are. In which areas are you not performing to the best of your ability?

1. _____

_____

2. _____

_____

3. _____

_____

Formulate a plan to reach your full potential in each area listed.

Six Months Review:

_____

_____

_____

Quotation Source Information:

_____

_____

_____

January 31
August 1

> "Surround yourself with the best people
> you can find, delegate authority, and don't
> interfere as long as the policy you've decided
> upon is being carried out."

Ronald Reagan

If you were to form a committee of five to run the important parts of your life, who would they be and why?

1. _____
   _____

2. _____
   _____

3. _____
   _____

4. _____
   _____

5. _____
   _____

Contact each today and create your own power team. Experience success at greater levels than before.

Six Months Review:

_____

_____
_____

Quotation Source Information:

_____

_____
_____

February 1
August 2

"By the structure of the world we often want,
at the sudden occurrence of a grave tempest,
to change the helmsman—to replace the pilot
of the calm by the pilot of the storm."

Walter Bagehot

Generally, a man is not for all seasons. We have leaders in depression and war as well as leaders in peace and prosperity. Make a list of your favorite leaders for each situation. Why did you select each leader?

_____
_____
_____
_____
_____

Six Months Review:

_____
_____
_____

Quotation Source Information:

_____
_____
_____

February 2
August 3

"A leader is one who knows where he wants to go,
and gets up and goes."

John Erskine

List people you feel are the best examples of the leader described in the quote:

1. _____

_____

2. _____

_____

3. _____

_____

What makes each person a leader?

Six Months Review:

_____

_____

_____

Quotation Source Information:

_____

_____

_____

February 3
August 4

Who speaks, sows; who listens, reaps.

Argentine Proverb

Today, choose a person and have a conversation with them where you listen more than you talk. Make note of your reaction.

_____
_____
_____
_____
_____

Six Months Review:

_____
_____
_____

Quotation Source Information:

_____
_____
_____

February 4
August 5

"The older I get the less I listen to what people say
and the more I look at what they do."

Andrew Carnegie

The best leaders lead by example, even when they may not even be in a leadership situation. List three people that are the best examples of leadership:

1. _____
   _____

2. _____
   _____

3. _____
   _____

What makes each unique?

Six Months Review:

_____
_____
_____

Quotation Source Information:

_____
_____
_____

February 5
August 6

"A really great man is known by three signs: generosity in design, humanity in the execution, moderation in success."

Otto von Bismark

Do you agree with the great man? _____

Why or why not?

_____
_____
_____
_____
_____

How have you personally shown these qualities in your actions?

_____
_____
_____
_____
_____

Six Months Review:

_____
_____
_____

Quotation Source Information:

_____
_____
_____

February 6
August 7

"There would be nothing to frighten you if you refuse to be afraid."

Mahatma Gandhi

Self-discipline should be a characteristic of both followers and leaders. Pick three of your personal weaknesses and improve upon them.

Weakness: _____

Action plan: _____

_____

Weakness: _____

Action plan: _____

_____

Weakness: _____

Action plan: _____

_____

Six Months Review:

_____

_____

_____

Quotation Source Information:

_____

_____

_____

February 7
August 8

"The time is always right to do what is right."

Martin Luther King, Jr.

Review your last three not so insignificant decisions. Did you do the right thing? Write your comments in the space below.

1. _____
   _____

2. _____
   _____

3. _____
   _____

Six Months Review:

_____
_____
_____

Quotation Source Information:

_____
_____
_____

February 8
August 9

"Men are often capable of greater things than they perform."

Horace Walpole

We all have so much unused or underutilized potential. Reasons may range from esteem issues, discovery, training or even laziness. In which areas do you feel that you have much more potential that is not being used to its full extent?

1. _____

   _____

2. _____

   _____

3. _____

   _____

Write an action plan to utilize your unused potential in each area.

Six Months Review:

_____

_____

_____

Quotation Source Information:

_____

_____

_____

February 9
August 10

"Self-command is the main elegance."

Ralph Waldo Emerson

How can you improve your self-control? Pick three areas, develop an improvement plan, and execute on the plan.

1. _____
   _____

2. _____
   _____

3. _____
   _____

Six Months Review:

_____
_____
_____

Quotation Source Information:

_____
_____
_____

February 10
August 11

"Success is simply an idea away. For achievement has its beginning in the idea and accomplishment with the idea being properly executed."

Richard Possett

Have you ever seen or heard something realizing that you had that same idea at another time in your life? List your best original ideas:

1. _____
   _____

2. _____
   _____

3. _____
   _____

Select one idea and write an action plan to develop that idea and do at least one thing today to see that idea become a reality.

Six Months Review:

_____
_____
_____

Quotation Source Information:

_____
_____
_____

February 11
August 12

"Are you daily cultivating leadership skills through appropriate books, tapes, CD's, videos, seminars, and mentors?"

Peter Biadasz

We live in an age where there are an amazing amount of informational resources available to us. List the leadership resources available in the following areas based on recommendations from the best leaders that you know:

Books: _____

Tapes: _____

C.D.'s: _____

Videos: _____

Seminars: _____

Mentors: _____

Write an action plan to obtain the resources that you listed that you do not yet own. Obtain one of the resources today. Register for one seminar and contact a mentor today.

Six Months Review:

_____

_____

_____

Quotation Source Information:

_____

_____

_____

February 12
August 13

"Each of us makes his own weather, determines the color of the skies in the emotional universe which he inhabits."

Fulton J. Sheen

Positive thinking creates self-fulfilling prophecies. What are your three weaknesses of attitude and positive thinking? Make a plan to convert these faults into talents.

1. _____
_____

2. _____
_____

3. _____
_____

Six Months Review:

_____
_____
_____

Quotation Source Information:

_____
_____
_____

February 13
August 14

> "Passion is an extreme, compelling emotion;
> an intense emotional drive or excitement."

Daniel Webster

We all have interests we feel very strongly about. List three things you are very passionate about:

1. _____

   _____

2. _____

   _____

3. _____

   _____

How can each passion be developed to its fullest potential?

Six Months Review:

_____

_____

_____

Quotation Source Information:

_____

_____

_____

February 14
August 15

"It's not that I'm so smart; it's just that
I stay with problems longer."

Albert Einstein

Persistence is often the key to success. Leaders often teach persistence by example. What are your most common excuses used to quit when problems arise?

1. _____
   _____

2. _____
   _____

3. _____
   _____

How can each excuse be dismissed and conquered?
1. _____
   _____

2. _____
   _____

3. _____
   _____

Six Months Review:

_____

_____

_____

Quotation Source Information:

_____

_____

_____

February 15
August 16

"The art of leadership is saying no, not yes.
It is very easy to say yes."

Tony Blair

Identify some incidences where you said *yes* because it was easier.

1. _____

   _____

2. _____

   _____

3. _____

   _____

Name some episodes where you said *no*.

1. _____

   _____

2. _____

   _____

3. _____

   _____

Recall how each event made you feel.

Six Months Review:

_____

_____

_____

Quotation Source Information:

_____

_____

_____

February 16
August 17

Ask the experienced rather than the learned.

Arabian Proverb

It is easier for us to accept information if we feel that the informer has walked the walk, not just talked the talk. List the most experienced leaders you know:

1. _____

   _____

2. _____

   _____

3. _____

   _____

Contact each today and learn how they became such experienced leaders. Record what you learn.

Six Months Review:

_____
_____
_____

Quotation Source Information:

_____
_____
_____

February 17
August 18

"Sometimes being blind enables you to see better
than those who have sight. People
who can see, often don't."

The Blog

When you look at a situation, what do you normally see? Is it a problem
or an opportunity? Please recall your last encounter with a tough situation. How did you handle it?

_____

_____

_____

_____

_____

Six Months Review:

_____

_____

_____

Quotation Source Information:

_____

_____

_____

February 18
August 19

"Don't find fault, find a remedy."

Henry Ford

There are whiners and there are winners. What is your biggest complaint in your life?

_____
_____
_____
_____
_____

What is the solution?

_____
_____
_____
_____
_____

Six Months Review:

_____
_____
_____

Quotation Source Information:

_____
_____
_____

February 19
August 20

"The speed of the leader is the speed of the gang."

Mary Kay Ash

It is always nice to get it right, but isn't it nice to get it right, do it quickly and move onto the next thing? How can you increase your energy level?

1. _____

   _____

2. _____

   _____

3. _____

   _____

How can you energize those around you?

1. _____

   _____

2. _____

   _____

3. _____

   _____

Six Months Review:

_____

_____

_____

Quotation Source Information:

_____

_____

_____

February 20
August 21

"Give every man thy ear but few thy voice."

William Shakespeare

A good leader listens. Re-examine your last three staff/sales meetings. What was the key input from those meetings? Note them below:

_____
_____
_____
_____
_____

Six Months Review:

_____
_____
_____

Quotation Source Information:

_____
_____
_____

February 21
August 22

"I look to the future because that's where
I'm going to spend the rest of my life."

George Burns

Sometimes the future may seem uncertain. Name some things you need
to change in your life for you to have the future that your desire:

1. _____

_____

2. _____

_____

3. _____

_____

Write down what you will do today to ensure those changes take place.

Six Months Review:

_____

_____

_____

Quotation Source Information:

_____

_____

_____

February 22
August 23

"To reach a great height a person needs to have great depth."

The taller the building, the deeper the foundation needs to be. How can you increase your depth?

1. _____
   _____

2. _____
   _____

3. _____
   _____

Who are the deepest people that you know?

1. _____
   _____

2. _____
   _____

3. _____
   _____

What makes them so deep?

Six Months Review:

_____
_____
_____

February 23
August 24

"Yesterday ended last night."

Norman Vincent Peale

Can you forget the past? Make a note of three things from the recent past that are troublesome. Resolve to cleanse them from your mind through resolution, forgiveness, or resolve.

1. _____
   _____

2. _____
   _____

3. _____
   _____

Six Months Review:

_____
_____
_____

Quotation Source Information:

_____
_____
_____

February 24
August 25

The generous man enriches himself by giving;
the miser hoards himself poor.

Dutch Proverb

Give today! Give of yourself, your possessions, and your money. Write
down your actions and your feelings.

_____
_____
_____
_____
_____

Six Months Review:

_____
_____
_____

Quotation Source Information:

_____
_____
_____

February 25
August 26

"Leadership is the transference of vision."

Hal Reed

Leaders gain followers by sharing key information. This information is called their vision. It is comprised of what the task at hand is and how to complete the task. List those people you consider visionaries:

1. _____
   _____

2. _____
   _____

3. _____
   _____

How does each person communicate his or her vision for the future?

Six Months Review:

_____
_____
_____

Quotation Source Information:

_____
_____
_____

February 26
August 27

"Courage is what it takes to stand up and speak;
courage is also what it takes to sit down and listen."

Winston Churchill

Knowing you have something important to say and actually saying it are not always easy. How do you know when it is time to stand up and speak? How do you build up the courage to speak?

1. _____
   _____

2. _____
   _____

3. _____
   _____

Other than someone telling you it is time, list three ways that you may know when to sit down and listen:

1. _____
   _____

2. _____
   _____

3. _____
   _____

Six Months Review:

_____

_____

_____

Quotation Source Information:

_____

_____

_____

February 27
August 28

Everything passes; everything wears out;
everything breaks.

Polish Proverb

The proverb is speaking to change. How do you personally cope with
change in your life? When did you last encounter major change? How
did you deal with it? How did it make you feel?

_____

_____

_____

_____

_____

Six Months Review:

_____

_____

_____

Quotation Source Information:

_____

_____

_____

February 28
August 29

"Fortune favors the audacious."

Erasmus

Audacity has made princes and kings for fortune favors the brave. With audacity one can undertake anything. Recall a few events where you used personal courage to achieve the endeavor. Make a note on how this made you feel? Share your feelings with people.

_____
_____
_____
_____
_____

Six Months Review:

_____
_____
_____

Quotation Source Information:

_____
_____
_____

February 29
August 30

"All that we are is the result of what we thought.
The mind is everything. What we think, we become."

Buddha

Is it rose colored glasses. A cloud of doom or Mr. In-Between? What
does this reality mean to you? Define it below.

_____
_____
_____
_____
_____

Six Months Review:

_____
_____
_____

Quotation Source Information:

_____
_____
_____

March 1
August 31

Love me when I deserve it,
because that's when I really need it.

Swedish Proverb

You are charismatic when you make others feel good about themselves.
You are conceited when you are only concerned about how you feel.
Which are you? Think about it! Write down your discovery.

_____

_____

_____

_____

_____

Six Months Review:

_____

_____

_____

Quotation Source Information:

_____

_____

_____

March 2
September 1

"Three things in human life are important.
The first is to be kind. The second is to be kind.
And the third is to be kind."

William Wood

This quote speaks for itself. List the kindest people you know:

1. _____

_____

2. _____

_____

3. _____

_____

Let them know today how much you appreciate their kindness. Record highlights of the conversations. List people that you will be especially kind to today:

1. _____

_____

2. _____

_____

3. _____

_____

Record the highlight of those interactions.

Six Months Review:

_____

_____

_____

Quotation Source Information:

_____

_____

_____

March 3
September 2

"If you fully stretch yourself beyond your conscious level of confidence, you will accelerate the development of your competence."

Richard Possett

Self-confidence and courage go hand-in-hand with effective leadership. High levels help you get things done when they really need doing.

Gauge your personal level of self-confidence.

_____
_____
_____
_____
_____

Ask a trusted friend to do the same.

_____
_____
_____
_____
_____

Six Months Review:

_____
_____
_____

Quotation Source Information:

_____
_____
_____

March 4
September 3

"Use the talents you possess."

Henry Van Dyke

We all have things we do exceptionally well. List your greatest talents:

1. _____

_____

2. _____

_____

3. _____

_____

4. _____

_____

5. _____

_____

List one way that you can further develop each talent.

Six Months Review:

_____

_____

_____

Quotation Source Information:

_____

_____

_____

March 5
September 4

"A strong passion for any object will ensure success, for the desire of the end will point out the means."

William Hazlitt

Write your job description. Do you feel any passion in the text? If so, note them below. If not, what are you going to do about it?

_____

_____

_____

_____

_____

Six Months Review:

_____

_____

_____

Quotation Source Information:

_____

_____

_____

March 6
September 5

"Our main business is not to see what lies dimly at a distance, but to do what lies clear at hand."

Thomas Carlyle

What are the main pressing issues in your life that give you discomfort? Make a note of each and in the next three days focus on resolving each one.

_____

_____

_____

_____

_____

Six Months Review:

_____

_____

Quotation Source Information:

_____

_____

_____

March 7
September 6

> "He who reigns within himself and rules his passions, desires, and fears is more than a king."

John Milton

The only thing we can control with some assurance is ourselves. Self-control is a good leadership trait. List instances in which you have demonstrated self-control:

1. _____
   _____

2. _____
   _____

3. _____
   _____

In each instance, how did you maintain self-control?

Six Months Review:

_____
_____
_____

Quotation Source Information:

_____
_____
_____

March 8
September 7

"We all have dreams. But in order to make dreams into reality, it takes an awful lot of determination, dedication, self-discipline and effort."

Jessie Owens

What are your dreams?
_____
_____

What characteristics do you believe are necessary to make your dreams come true?
_____
_____

Do you possess those traits?
_____
_____

How are you working on actualizing your dreams?
_____
_____

Six Months Review:
_____
_____
_____

Quotation Source Information:
_____
_____
_____

March 9
September 8

"The wisdom of life consists in the elimination of nonessentials."

Lin Yutang

As we mature or as circumstances change we may realize that many things we hold dear to us really are not very important. List the most non-essential things in your life:

1. _____
   _____

2. _____
   _____

3. _____
   _____

In a way that is legal, moral and ethical, eliminate each item from your life.

Six Months Review:

_____
_____
_____

Quotation Source Information:

_____
_____
_____

March 10
September 9

"To succeed in the world, it is much more necessary to possess the penetration to discern who is a fool than to discover who is a clever man."

Talleyrand

The sixth and sensible senses are key factors to good leadership. Who is the best leader that you know?

_____

Do they possess these qualities? _____

Visit with them and ask how they honed these traits. Note your discoveries:

_____

_____

_____

_____

_____

Six Months Review:

_____

_____

_____

Quotation Source Information:

_____

_____

_____

March 11
September 10

"There is no way to make people like change.
You can only make them feel less threatened by it."

Frederick Hayes

No one likes change. Yet in life things change daily. Change will happen and it will happen to you and those around you. In what ways can you assist yourself and others in helping to alleviate the threat felt by change?

1. _____
   _____

2. _____
   _____

3. _____
   _____

4. _____
   _____

5. _____
   _____

Master each technique today!!!

Six Months Review:

_____
_____
_____

Quotation Source Information:

_____
_____
_____

March 12
September 11

"Mentor: Someone who helps another person become what that person aspires to be."

M. S. Gladstone

List your most valuable mentors. Contact each to express heartfelt appreciation:

1. _____

_____

2. _____

_____

3. _____

_____

Who would you like to mentor?

1. _____

_____

2. _____

_____

3. _____

_____

Contact each today to begin the mentoring process.

Six Months Review:

_____

_____

_____

Quotation Source Information:

_____

_____

_____

March 13
September 12

"Without courage, all other virtues lose their meaning."

Winston Churchill

What makes a person courageous? Take a few minutes to think about your answer. Note your thoughts:

_____
_____
_____
_____
_____

Six Months Review:

_____
_____
_____

Quotation Source Information:

_____
_____
_____

March 14
September 13

"The most important thing in communication
is to hear what isn't being said."

Peter F. Drucker

We have non-verbal communications, the half-truths, and the things that go unsaid. Go back to recent situations and identify an example of each event and comment on them.

Non-verbal communications:

_____

_____

Half-truths:

_____

_____

Things that go unsaid:

_____

_____

Six Months Review:

_____

_____

_____

Quotation Source Information:

_____

_____

_____

March 15
September 14

"Until you value yourself, you won't value your time.
Until you value your time,
you will not do anything with it."

M. Scott Peck

We all have different ways to measure value. In which ways do you value yourself?

1. _____
   _____

2. _____
   _____

3. _____
   _____

How do you show value to your time?

1. _____
   _____

2. _____
   _____

3. _____
   _____

Six Months Review:

_____

_____

_____

Quotation Source Information:

_____

_____

_____

March 16
September 15

"We are cups, constantly and quietly being filled.
The trick is, knowing how to tip ourselves over and
let the beautiful stuff out."

Ray Bradbury

You know the very best you posses inwardly. How can you express the very best of who you know you are?

1. _____
   _____

2. _____
   _____

3. _____
   _____

Six Months Review:

_____
_____
_____

Quotation Source Information:

_____
_____
_____

March 17
September 16

"Do not say a little in many words but
a great deal in a few."

Pythagoras

Are you wordy or succinct when you write a memorandum or letter?
Write down three ways in which you could make your written word
more effective in communicating your thoughts.

1. _____

   _____

2. _____

   _____

3. _____

   _____

Six Months Review:

_____

_____

_____

Quotation Source Information:

_____

_____

_____

March 18
September 17

"Great minds have purposes, others have wishes."

Washington Irving

The question is…How bad do you want it? Are the things you want in your life merely wishes or committed goals? List three of your objectives in life. Think about them and determine if they are wishes or goals.

1. _____

   _____

2. _____

   _____

3. _____

   _____

Six Months Review:

_____

_____

_____

Quotation Source Information:

_____

_____

_____

March 19
September 18

"The acquisition and refining of leadership skills is a lifelong process."

Peter Biadasz

There is no such person as the perfect leader. Variables exist in the people and the circumstances a leader may find him or her in. Understanding this, in which leadership skills are you lacking?

1. _____
   _____

2. _____
   _____

3. _____
   _____

How will you acquire each skill that you lack?

List leadership skills you have that need refining:

1. _____
   _____

2. _____
   _____

3. _____
   _____

How will you refine each leadership skill?

Six Months Review:

_____

_____

_____

Quotation Source Information:

_____

_____

_____

March 20
September 19

> "Never grow a wishbone, daughter,
> where your backbone ought to be."

Clementine Paddleford

The phrase speaks to the courage of our convictions. What are your personal views on leadership? Are you committed to them?

_____
_____
_____
_____
_____

Six Months Review:

_____
_____
_____

Quotation Source Information:

_____
_____
_____

March 21
September 20

"Unless we are willing to help a person overcome his faults, there is little value in pointing them out."

Robert Hastings

Leadership is about giving. In which ways can you help others overcome their deficiencies in ways that build them up, not tear them down?

1. _____
   _____

2. _____
   _____

3. _____
   _____

Who has helped you the same way and how did they help you?

_____
_____
_____
_____
_____

Six Months Review:

_____
_____
_____

Quotation Source Information:

_____
_____
_____

March 22
September 21

"There are two kinds of strength, one brings out the strength of the other, helps it to be born.
The other kind imposes its own strength and weakens those who submit to it."

Anais Nin

Great leaders assist in making more great leaders. In which ways have leaders in your life nurtured your strengths?

1. _____
_____

2. _____
_____

3. _____
_____

4. _____
_____

5. _____
_____

Following the example already set for you, whose strength will you help nurture today? _____

What is your plan?

_____
_____

Six Months Review:

_____
_____
_____

Quotation Source Information:

_____
_____
_____

March 23
September 22

"I used to say of him [Napoleon] that his presence
on the field made the difference of forty
thousand men."

Duke of Wellington

What is your style of leadership?

_____
_____
_____
_____
_____

How does it make a difference on the field of life?

_____
_____
_____
_____
_____

Six Months Review:

_____
_____
_____

Quotation Source Information:

_____
_____
_____

March 24
September 23

"The final test of a leader is that he leaves behind him in other men the conviction and the will to carry on."

Walter Lippmann

Leaders understand that success without a successor is not true success. Passing on your closely held convictions is a part of the process. Do you have the courage of your convictions?_____

How have you passed your convictions onto others?

1. _____
   _____

2. _____
   _____

3. _____
   _____

Six Months Review:

_____
_____
_____

Quotation Source Information:

_____
_____
_____

March 25
September 24

"Don't smother each other,
no one can grow in the shade."

Leo Buscaglis

Many people are hired because of their independence and their ability to work with little supervision. Yet many times these same people are eventually managed by someone that is so *hands on* that the employee feels smothered and in the long term is not as productive while experiencing high job dissatisfaction. How can you give someone space yet still nurture them?

1. _____

   _____

2. _____

   _____

3. _____

   _____

Six Months Review:

_____

_____

_____

Quotation Source Information:

_____

_____

_____

March 26
September 25

"If you wish to make a man your enemy,
tell him simply, 'You are wrong.'
This method works every time."

Henry C. Link

Note creative yet effective ways that you can **constructively** inform others that they may be not right or not correct:

1. _____

_____

2. _____

_____

3. _____

_____

Six Months Review:

_____

_____

_____

Quotation Source Information:

_____

_____

_____

March 27
September 26

"No man is free who is not a master of himself."

Epictetus

Self-control is the trait that leaders use to plan, organize, oversee and adjust. Can you recall the last time you lost your self-control? What was the situation? If need be, go make amends.

_____

_____

_____

_____

_____

Six Months Review:

_____

_____

_____

Quotation Source Information:

_____

_____

_____

March 28
September 27

"All is change; all yields its place and goes."

Euripides

Do you agree with the above phrase? _____

What does it mean to you?

_____
_____
_____
_____
_____

Six Months Review:

_____
_____
_____

Quotation Source Information:

_____
_____
_____

March 29
September 28

"It's simply bushido my good man, it is simply bushido."

Vanposetski

In the space below, define your personal system of morals or code of moral conduct. Call it your ethics statement or declaration.

_____

_____

_____

_____

_____

Six Months Review:

_____

_____

_____

Quotation Source Information:

_____

_____

_____

March 30
September 29

"Those who stand for nothing, fall for anything."

Alex Hamilton

Character is the distinctive trait, essential quality and pattern of behavior found in an individual. It is the essence of leadership. List three traits that make for a good character:

1. _____

_____

2. _____

_____

3. _____

_____

Six Months Review:

_____

_____

_____

Quotation Source Information:

_____

_____

_____

March 31
September 30

A kind word is like a spring day.

Russian Proverb

We all like to receive kind words, no matter how happy or sad we may be. Who will you share a kind word with today?

1. _____

   _____

2. _____

   _____

3. _____

   _____

Six Months Review:

_____

_____

_____

Quotation Source Information:

_____

_____

_____

April 1
October 1

"Vitality shows not only in the ability to persist,
but in the ability to start over."

F. Scott Fitzgerald

Perseverance is a commendable trait, but it can be over done at times.
Are you involved in something that has taken too long to finish? Should
you just start over? Why or Why not?

_____

_____

_____

_____

_____

Six Months Review:

_____

_____

_____

Quotation Source Information:

_____

_____

_____

April 2
October 2

"Don't waste time calculating your chances of success and failure. Just fix your aim and begin."

Guan Yin Tzu

Concentration and focus are keys to accomplishment. Recall the last time you took your eyes off the target. How did you readjust the aim?

_____

_____

_____

_____

_____

Six Months Review:

_____

_____

_____

Quotation Source Information:

_____

_____

_____

April 3
October 3

"When anger rises, think of the consequences."

Confucius

Many times we think of the consequences of inappropriate anger after the incident has passed. List three things that are guaranteed to make you angry:

1. _____
   _____

2. _____
   _____

3. _____
   _____

What are the negative consequences of anger for each circumstance? How can you avoid anger in each circumstance?

Six Months Review:
_____
_____
_____

Quotation Source Information:
_____
_____
_____

April 4
October 4

"Yes, there is Nirvana: it is in leading your sheep to a green pasture, and in putting your child to sleep, and in writing the last line of your poem."

Kahil Gibran

In the hurly-burly of daily life, we often forget the small and what appears to be insignificant. Take some time today and note a couple of these positive events. Make a big deal about them. This is how we count our blessings.

_____
_____
_____
_____
_____

Six Months Review:

_____
_____
_____

Quotation Source Information:

_____
_____
_____

April 5
October 5

"He has the heart of an oak, but feet of clay."

Vanposetski

The person we are talking about has the appearance of having a strong and courageous nature, but has the fundamental flaw of lacking personal courage. Think about your character. Do you feel you have any inadequacies that may need repairing? Make a list and a plan to remodel you:

_____

_____

_____

_____

_____

Six Months Review:

_____

_____

_____

Quotation Source Information:

_____

_____

_____

April 6
October 6

"Talent develops in quiet places, character in the full current of human life."

Goethe

What one thing would you like to learn about your character? Note it below and go into the world and discover the answer. Make a record of your discovery:

_____

_____

_____

_____

_____

Six Months Review:

_____

_____

_____

Quotation Source Information:

_____

_____

_____

April 7
October 7

"He that cannot obey cannot command."

15th Century Saying

A good leader is also a good follower. The experience of being under orders teaches one how they should be given. Recall a significant experience in your life where you may have had difficulty taking orders. What life lessons did you learn from that episode?

_____

_____

_____

_____

_____

Six Months Review:

_____

_____

_____

Quotation Source Information:

_____

_____

_____

April 8
October 8

"The fish always stinks from the head downwards."

16th Century Saying

The meaning is that as the freshness of a dead fish can be judged from the condition of it head, any corruption in a country or organization will be manifested first in its leaders. Have you had any personal or professional experiences with misguided leadership? If so, recall below the actions and character of the leaders. If not, be on the lookout for such conduct.

_____

_____

_____

_____

_____

Six Months Review:

_____

_____

_____

Quotation Source Information:

_____

_____

_____

April 9
October 9

"The difference between motivation and manipulation is all in the motive of the mover."

POZ

A leader has the ability to incite people to action for bilateral benefit. Name the chief ways in which you inspire others to get things done. Are you motivating or manipulating?

1. _____
   _____

2. _____
   _____

3. _____
   _____

Six Months Review:
_____
_____
_____

Quotation Source Information:
_____
_____
_____

April 10
October 10

"When you have decided what you believe,
what you feel must be done,
have the courage to stand alone and be counted."

Eleanor Roosevelt

What are your living life beliefs? Develop a bill of beliefs and write them
down in the space below:

_____

_____

_____

_____

_____

Are you truly committed to those principles?

Six Months Review:

_____

_____

_____

Quotation Source Information:

_____

_____

_____

April 11
October 11

"Nothing indicates the soundness of a man's judgment so much as knowing how to choose between two disadvantages."

Seneca

Some say adversity defines character. Others, adverse decision making. A leader must posses both qualities. When last faced with adversity, how did you decide?

_____

_____

_____

_____

_____

In hindsight, was it the best decision? What lessons did you learn?

_____

_____

_____

Six Months Review:

_____

_____

_____

Quotation Source Information:

_____

_____

_____

April 12
October 12

"The only real training for leadership is leadership."

Anthony Jay

Sometimes the best way to learn responsibility is to take on responsibility. What leadership positions do you desire?

1. _____

   _____

2. _____

   _____

3. _____

   _____

Circle which is most important to you and write an action plan that you can begin today in order to earn that position of leadership.

_____

_____

_____

_____

_____

Six Months Review:

_____

_____

_____

Quotation Source Information:

_____

_____

_____

April 13
October 13

"I attribute my success to this:
I never gave or took an excuse."

Florence Nightingale

We are responsible for our own actions. While we cannot stop others from making excuses, we can control which excuses we accept or make. Which excuses do you commonly use?

1. _____
   _____

2. _____
   _____

3. _____
   _____

Never use these or any other excuses again.

Six Months Review:

_____
_____
_____

Quotation Source Information:

_____
_____
_____

April 14
October 14

"Wise men learn by others men's mistakes, fools by their own."

H.G. Bohn

It is easy to learn from others mistakes. They will brag about them like fools or write and teach about them so that others can learn from them. List people of great success whose biographies you will buy today to learn from their mistakes:

1. _____
   _____

2. _____
   _____

3. _____
   _____

Write what you learned from each biography.

_____
_____
_____
_____
_____

Six Months Review:

_____

_____

_____

Quotation Source Information:

_____

_____

_____

April 15
October 15

"Never for the sake of peace and quiet
deny your own experience or convictions."

Dag Hammarskjold

If you speak the truth, it may set you free, but not necessarily endear you to others. Leaders say what they mean and mean what they say. Note those honest beliefs of yours that may seem as not being politically correct and speak to others about them.

_____

_____

_____

_____

_____

Six Months Review:

_____

_____

_____

Quotation Source Information:

_____

_____

_____

April 16
October 16

"Eagle-eyed toward others and moles to ourselves."

Vanposetski

To understand yourself better, define the above statement. What does it mean for and about you?

_____
_____
_____
_____
_____

Six Months Review:

_____
_____
_____

Quotation Source Information:

_____
_____
_____

April 17
October 17

"Be the change you wish to see in the world."

Mahatma Gandhi

It is so easy to complain about what we want changed in the world in which we live. List things that you would like to see changed in the world:

1. _____
   _____

2. _____
   _____

3. _____
   _____

Circle which item is most important to you and write an action plan that you can begin today to start effecting that change.

_____
_____
_____
_____
_____

Six Months Review:

_____
_____
_____

Quotation Source Information:

_____
_____
_____

April 18
October 18

"You can't build a reputation on what you are going to do."

Henry Ford

We all know someone that always has a great plan for his or her life but never follows through to complete or maybe even start the plan. What are you presently doing to enhance your reputation?

1. _____

_____

2. _____

_____

3. _____

_____

Six Months Review:

_____

_____

_____

Quotation Source Information:

_____

_____

_____

April 19
October 19

"A decision is the action an executive must take
when he has information so incomplete that the
answer does not suggest itself."

Arthur Radford

We live in an age of endless information but we never seem to get the
right and often necessary information when we need it. How can you
receive more complete information when making a decision?

1. _____

_____

2. _____

_____

3. _____

_____

4. _____

_____

5. _____

_____

Six Months Review:

_____

_____

_____

Quotation Source Information:

_____

_____

_____

April 20
October 20

"The ability to speak eloquently is not to be confused with having something to say."

Michael P. Hart

Have you ever had to listen to someone who very eloquently said nothing? It is a waste of both your time as well as theirs. Ask those close to you to evaluate your speaking skills, both in content and presentation. Record your findings below.

_____
_____
_____
_____
_____

Utilize this newfound knowledge to become a better speaker and presenter, in both small and large settings.

Six Months Review:

_____
_____
_____

Quotation Source Information:

_____
_____
_____

April 21
October 21

"Kindness in words creates confidence."

Lao-tzu

Helping others is an example of right and proper leadership. It need not be money; it need not been food and clothing; it just can be a helping hand. Note one person today and go help them in a way they will not discover:

_____

_____

_____

_____

_____

That is true kindness.

Six Months Review:

_____

_____

_____

Quotation Source Information:

_____

_____

_____

April 22
October 22

"Great minds have great purposes, others have wishes."

Washington Irving

Everyone is here to achieve a great purpose. What is your purpose?

_____

What are you doing to turn your wishes into reality to fulfill your purpose?

1. _____
   _____

2. _____
   _____

3. _____
   _____

Six Months Review:

_____
_____
_____

Quotation Source Information:

_____
_____
_____

April 23
October 23

"The sole life which a man can lose is that
which he is living at the moment."

Marcus Aurelius

Right now make a list of everything you want to accomplish within the
next 24 hours:

_____

_____

_____

_____

_____

Now go do them!!!!

Six Months Review:

_____

_____

_____

Quotation Source Information:

_____

_____

_____

April 24
October 24

"A man's character is his fate."

Heraclitus

Leaders have the conviction and core of character. What does character personally mean to you? In the space provided below write your personal character declaration and definition.

_____
_____
_____
_____
_____

Six Months Review:

_____
_____
_____

Quotation Source Information:

_____
_____
_____

April 25
October 25

"The hardest arithmetic to master is that which
enables us to count our blessings."

Eric Hoffer

Sometimes we get so busy working to get what we want we forget to be thankful for what we have. In your life, what are you truly grateful for?

1. _____

_____

2. _____

_____

3. _____

_____

4. _____

_____

5. _____

_____

Next to each item listed, write the name of someone that you will share each blessing, either verbally or in some other creative way.

Six Months Review:

_____

_____

_____

Quotation Source Information:

_____

_____

_____

April 26
October 26

"Seeing the invisible is true vision.
Hearing silence is acute listening.
Both are the skills of a leader."

Richard Possett

A leader has vision and listens to others. What about you? Can you visualize before you act or create? If yes, great! If no, develop a plan to strengthen this area.

_____
_____
_____
_____
_____

Six Months Review:

_____
_____
_____

Quotation Source Information:

_____
_____
_____

April 27
October 27

"See no evil, hear no evil, speak no evil"

The Three Wise Monkeys

The phrase is a reminder not to be so snoopy, so nosy and so gossipy. These tenets make for a good attitude. All of them are good leadership qualities. Rate yourself, one being bad and ten being good, on these leader characteristics.

See no evil— _____

Hear no evil—_____

Speak no evil—_____

How can you improve for the positive in each area?

_____
_____
_____
_____
_____

Six Months Review:

_____
_____
_____

Quotation Source Information:

_____
_____
_____

April 28
October 28

"Guido the plumber and Michelangelo
obtained their marble from the same quarry,
but what each saw in the marble made the difference
between a nobleman's sink and a brilliant sculpture."

Bob Kall

Leaders not only develop their own potential, but also discover the hidden potential in those around them. How do you identify the potential that lies within another individual?

1. _____
   _____

2. _____
   _____

3. _____
   _____

Six Months Review:

_____
_____
_____

Quotation Source Information:

_____
_____
_____

April 29
October 29

"Don't just say it, do it!"

Peter Biadasz

Nothing is more powerful than leadership by example. List those you admire for the example they have displayed for you.

1. _____
   _____

2. _____
   _____

3. _____
   _____

Contact each to learn their secret to effective leadership. Note what they share with you.

Six Months Review:

_____
_____
_____

April 30
October 30

"Courage is more exhilarating than fear and in the long run it is easier. We do not have to become heroes over night. Just a step at a time, meeting each thing that comes up, seeing it is not as dreadful as it appeared, discovering we have the strength to stare it down."

Eleanor Roosevelt

We all have known or heard about others that have overcome something to achieve a greater goal. Who are the most courageous people that you have met?

1. _____
   _____

2. _____
   _____

3. _____
   _____

What made each so courageous?

Six Months Review:

_____
_____
_____

Quotation Source Information:

_____
_____
_____

May 1
October 31

"Lots of people talk to animals...
Not very many listen, though... That's the problem."

The Tao of Pooh

Listening is a real skill and a good leadership quality. List ways you might improve your listening skills:

1. _____

   _____

2. _____

   _____

3. _____

   _____

Develop a plan to practice your targeted procedures.

_____
_____
_____
_____
_____

Six Months Review:

_____
_____
_____

Quotation Source Information:

_____
_____
_____

May 2
November 1

If you think you're leading and no one is following you, then you're only taking a walk.

Leadership Proverb

What leadership qualities do you feel are important in a leader so that others will follow?

1. _____
   _____

2. _____
   _____

3. _____
   _____

4. _____
   _____

5. _____
   _____

Next to each quality, write an action plan to develop each quality in you.

Six Months Review:

_____
_____
_____

Quotation Source Information:

_____
_____
_____

May 3
November 2

"Life's most persistent and urgent question is,
'What are you doing for others?'"

Martin Luther King, Jr.

Leading is giving. What things do you do daily for others?

1. _____
   _____

2. _____
   _____

3. _____
   _____

Six Months Review:
_____
_____
_____

Quotation Source Information:
_____
_____
_____

May 4
November 3

"A great leader is married to organization, vision, and mentorship and gives each of these balanced attention."

Terry Miller

Achieving balance in life can be challenge. Can you name leaders who keep the balance stated above?

1. _____
   _____

2. _____
   _____

3. _____
   _____

How does each leader maintain the balance of the three parts?

_____
_____
_____
_____
_____

Six Months Review:

_____
_____
_____

Quotation Source Information:

_____
_____
_____

May 5
November 4

"I must govern the clock, not be governed by it."

Golda Meir

We all have the same 24 hours everyday. Managing those hours effectively and efficiently is key to powerful leadership. What are your strongest time management practices?

1. _____

_____

2. _____

_____

3. _____

_____

How can you improve on each practice listed?

_____
_____
_____
_____
_____

Six Months Review:

_____
_____
_____

Quotation Source Information:

_____
_____
_____

May 6
November 5

"A leader is a dealer in hope."

Napoleon Bonaparte

A true test of a leader is to lead when all hope is lost. Note ways that a leader can instill hope in those that he or she leads:

1. _____
   _____

2. _____
   _____

3. _____
   _____

Six Months Review:

_____
_____
_____

Quotation Source Information:

_____
_____
_____

May 7
November 6

"Most great people have attained their greatest success just one step beyond their greatest failure."

Napoleon Hill

Everyone needs to perform at a high level to succeed. Examine your standards. Develop an outline of more exacting self-expectations for a level of personal achievement.

_____

_____

_____

_____

_____

Six Months Review:

_____

_____

_____

Quotation Source Information:

_____

_____

_____

May 8
November 7

"You do not lead by hitting people over the head— that's assault, not leadership."

Dwight D. Eisenhower

There are many styles of leadership, some more effective than others. Which leadership styles have been the most effective when you are being led, and when you are leading?

When you are being led:

1. _____
   _____

2. _____
   _____

3. _____
   _____

When you are leading:

1. _____
   _____

2. _____
   _____

3. _____
   _____

Six Months Review:

_____

_____

_____

Quotation Source Information:

_____

_____

_____

May 9
November 8

"I am not afraid of storms
for I am learning how to sail my ship."

Louisa May Alcott

Sometimes the best way to learn is to go through rough times. Are you always easy to lead? You may recall some headaches you have given leaders in your past. Now you know you are a leader, note people that you have had or are having difficulty in leading:

Name: _____

_____

Name: _____

_____

Name: _____

_____

List what skills you will need to acquire and how you will acquire those skills to better lead these individuals.

Six Months Review:

_____

_____

_____

Quotation Source Information:

_____

_____

_____

May 10
November 9

> "Leaders make it clear…mistakes give us feedback
> and tell us what to do next."

Warren Bennis

Hopefully, when we make a mistake we learn from it and do not repeat it. List some mistakes you have made and what you learned from each mistake:

1. _____
   _____

2. _____
   _____

3. _____
   _____

How do you ensure that you do not repeat a mistake?

_____
_____
_____
_____

Six Months Review:

_____
_____
_____

Quotation Source Information:

_____
_____
_____

May 11
November 10

"Leadership is not magnetic personality/that can just as well be a glib tongue. It is not making friends and influencing people/that is flattery. Leadership is lifting a person's vision to higher sights, the raising of a person's performance to a higher standard, the building of a personality beyond its normal limitations."

Peter Drucker

Think about someone you personally recognize as a true leader. Visit with them and ask then how they take people to higher levels of performance. Note their answers below:

_____
_____
_____
_____
_____

Six Months Review:

_____
_____
_____

Quotation Source Information:

_____
_____
_____

May 12
November 11

"Success is dependent on effort."

Sophocles

We know when we are giving the best effort we are capable of. How can you increase the effort you put forth daily?

1. _____
   _____

2. _____
   _____

3. _____
   _____

Six Months Review:

_____
_____
_____

Quotation Source Information:

_____
_____
_____

May 13
November 12

"'No comment' is a splendid expression.
I am using it again and again."

Winston Churchill

Sometimes things are better left unsaid. List instances in which you clearly said too much:

1. _____
   _____

2. _____
   _____

3. _____
   _____

Record how you will, in the future, be wiser in what you say, how you say it, now much you say, and knowing when it is best to say nothing.

_____
_____
_____
_____
_____

Six Months Review:

_____
_____
_____

Quotation Source Information:

_____
_____
_____

"Wisdom is the reward you get for a lifetime of listening when you'd have preferred to talk."

Doug Larson

Develop three new questions that you may ask someone whom you just met to engage him or her in a conversation creating some common interests.

1. _____

   _____

2. _____

   _____

3. _____

   _____

Six Months Review:

_____

_____

_____

Quotation Source Information:

_____

_____

_____

May 15
November 14

"Don't let your will roar when
your power only whispers."

Thomas Fuller

It is easy to have lofty ambitions without the means to meet those plans.
How can you increase your personal and professional power?

Personal power:

1. _____

_____

2. _____

_____

3. _____

_____

Professional power:

1. _____

_____

2. _____

_____

3. _____

_____

Six Months Review:

_____

_____

_____

Quotation Source Information:

_____

_____

_____

May 16
November 15

"Hold yourself responsible for a higher standard than anybody expects of you."

Henry Ward Beecher

A true leader leads in many areas, including expecting more from him or herself than anyone else could or would. In which areas of your life can you raise your standards?

1. _____

_____

2. _____

_____

3. _____

_____

4. _____

_____

5. _____

_____

Write one thing that you can do today to improve your standard in each area listed.

Six Months Review:

_____
_____
_____

Quotation Source Information:

_____
_____
_____

May 17
November 16

"What we see depends mainly on what we look for."

John Lubbock

We can always look for the good and/or the bad in people, places and things. Reflect on your outlook on life. Define it in the space below.

_____
_____
_____
_____
_____

Six Months Review:

_____
_____
_____

Quotation Source Information:

_____
_____
_____

May 18
November 17

"Leadership is based on inspiration, not domination; on cooperation, not intimidation."

William Wood

We have all had leaders that inspired us. We worked happily and diligently for those leaders. We have also had the dominating and intimidating leaders and shared in the fruits of those labors. You know which circumstance was the better. List ways that you can inspire others today to improve their day:

1. _____
   _____

2. _____
   _____

3. _____
   _____

What were the results of each inspiring act?

_____
_____
_____
_____
_____

Six Months Review:

_____

_____

_____

Quotation Source Information:

_____

_____

_____

May 19
November 18

"The first rule is to keep an untroubled spirit.
The second is to look things in the face
and know them for what they are."

Marcus Aurelius

Recognizing obstacles for what they really are is key in all situations. Anticipating problems is also important in peacefully finding solutions. There is a difference between reacting and responding to a challenging situation. What things have you had to face in life and conquer with courage?

1. _____

_____

2. _____

_____

3. _____

_____

How did you overcome each situation?

Six Months Review:

_____
_____
_____

Quotation Source Information:

_____
_____
_____

May 20
November 19

"Leadership is not about being nice.
It's about being right and being strong."

Paul Keating

True leadership is about much more than just strength and correctness.
Make your own list of leadership features:

_____

_____

_____

_____

_____

Six Months Review:

_____

_____

_____

Quotation Source Information:

_____

_____

_____

May 21
November 20

"Life is denied by lack of attention, whether it be to cleaning windows or trying to write a masterpiece."

Nadia Boulanger

Attention to detail is important in every endeavor, whether in our personal or professional lives.

On a scale of 1 to 10, with 10 being most attentive to detail, rate yourself:

_____

Ask three people that you trust to rate you: 1. _____ 2. _____ 3. _____

List three ways you can improve your attentiveness:
1. _____
   _____

2. _____
   _____

3. _____
   _____

Six Months Review:

_____
_____
_____

Quotation Source Information:

_____
_____
_____

May 22
November 21

"If a man hasn't discovered something he will die for, he isn't fit to live."

Martin Luther King, Jr.

What are you willing to die for? Think about it. Write down your answer:

_____
_____
_____
_____
_____

Do your actions match your words? _____

Six Months Review:

_____
_____
_____

Quotation Source Information:

_____
_____
_____

May 23
November 22

"The will to win is worthless if you do not have the will to prepare."

Thane Yost

It is amazing how much work goes into being an overnight success. List ways that you prepare daily to reach your full leadership potential:

1. _____

   _____

2. _____

   _____

3. _____

   _____

List next to each item someone that you can talk with today to better prepare in that area.

Six Months Review:

_____
_____
_____

Quotation Source Information:

_____
_____
_____

May 24
November 23

"Many receive advice, few profit by it."

Publilius Syrus

List the three best pieces of advice you have received in your life:
1. _____
   _____

2. _____
   _____

3. _____
   _____

Who will you share each piece of advice with today?
_____

Six Months Review:
_____
_____
_____

Quotation Source Information:
_____
_____
_____

May 25
November 24

"A team that has character doesn't need stimulation."

Tom Landry

Real true motivation is much more internal than external. How do you deal with self-motivation? Write down the ways and then discuss with a trusted friend or associate for clarity:

_____
_____
_____
_____
_____

Six Months Review:

_____
_____
_____

Quotation Source Information:

_____
_____
_____

May 26
November 25

"Only those means of security are good, are certain, are lasting, that depend on yourself and your vigor."

Machiavelli

Teamwork is important, but without self-reliance it would be impotent. The remedies simply and often lie within us. When was the last time you looked to yourself for the solution? Note your answer and how it made you feel:

_____

_____

_____

_____

_____

Six Months Review:

_____

_____

_____

Quotation Source Information:

_____

_____

_____

May 27
November 26

"You can only go as far as you push."

Unknown

Who do you trust to push and guide you to the next level of performance in the following areas?

Professional development:

_____

Personal development:

_____

Leadership skills:

_____

Your weakest area:

_____

Today contact each person listed and get one idea from each that you can begin with before you go to bed tonight.

Six Months Review:

_____

_____

_____

May 28
November 27

"An ape's an ape, a varlet's a varlet though they be clad in silk or scarlet."

16th Century Saying

This asserts that one's inward nature cannot be overcome by outward show. From your worldview, what is the mission of a leader? Write your leadership statement below:

_____
_____
_____
_____
_____

Six Months Review:

_____
_____
_____

Quotation Source Information:

_____
_____
_____

May 29
November 28

"Always position yourself for success."

Peter Biadasz

Whether we realize it or not, we can position or set ourselves up for failure or for success. Being the optimist, list ways in which you can predispose yourself to success in leadership:

_____

_____

_____

_____

_____

Go out and do them!!!

Six Months Review:

_____

_____

_____

Quotation Source Information:

_____

_____

_____

May 30
November 29

"Practice being excited."

Bill Foster

Attitude is truly contagious, both positive and negative. The greatest leaders have not only known what they were passionate about but are able to express that passion in positive ways to those that follow them. What truly excites you?

1. _____
   _____

2. _____
   _____

3. _____
   _____

4. _____
   _____

5. _____
   _____

Write how you can share those excitements with others. Also write how that excitement can carry over into other areas of your life.

Six Months Review:

_____

_____

_____

Quotation Source Information:

_____

_____

_____

May 31
November 30

"There is nothing more certain than the defeat of the man who gives up"

Former Cancer Patient

We all face challenges. How do you ensure you will not give up when things get rough?

1. _____

   _____

2. _____

   _____

3. _____

   _____

4. _____

   _____

5. _____

   _____

Six Months Review:

_____

_____

_____

Quotation Source Information:

_____

_____

_____

June 1
December 1

"Divide each difficulty into as many parts as is feasible and necessary to resolve it."

Rene Descartes

Completing complex tasks is an art form. What are three of the biggest challenges that you presently face?

1. _____
   _____

2. _____
   _____

3. _____
   _____

Break each item listed down into the smaller parts needed to satisfy each challenge.

Six Months Review:
_____
_____
_____

Quotation Source Information:
_____
_____
_____
_____

June 2
December 2

"You need to overcome the tug of people against you as you reach for high goals."

George S. Patton

They say that it is lonely at the top. List ways that you can keep looking up as you climb and not back at the people or weights that tug at you:

1. _____

   _____

2. _____

   _____

3. _____

   _____

Six Months Review:

_____

_____

_____

Quotation Source Information:

_____

_____

_____

June 3
December 3

"The Nelson Touch."

Lord Nelson

This is defined as a masterly or sympathetic approach to a problem used by the person in charge. Empathy and sympathy are good leadership qualities. Think of some examples of when you last utilized those features in solving an executive problem. Note the situation and outcome below.

1. _____
   _____

2. _____
   _____

3. _____
   _____

Six Months Review:

_____
_____
_____

Quotation Source Information:

_____
_____
_____

June 4
December 4

"Nature gives us one tongue and two ears so we could hear twice as much as we speak."

Epictetus

Good communication skills are essential for good leadership. In that light, what personal rules do you follow for listening to what others have to say? Reflect on them. Write them down:

_____
_____
_____
_____
_____

Do they need to be modified for better results?_____

Six Months Review:

_____
_____
_____

Quotation Source Information:

_____
_____
_____

June 5
December 5

"Nothing is more despicable than respect
based on fear."

Albert Camus

There are positive and negative ways to earn respect. List positive ways
to earn the respect of others:

1. _____
   _____

2. _____
   _____

3. _____
   _____

Practice each daily.

Six Months Review:

_____
_____
_____

Quotation Source Information:

_____
_____
_____

June 6
December 6

"I do not think much of a man who is not wiser
today than he was yesterday."

Abraham Lincoln

How can you increase your wisdom each day?

1. _____

_____

2. _____

_____

3. _____

_____

Share one thing you learn each day with a trusted person in your life.

Six Months Review:

_____

_____

_____

Quotation Source Information:

_____

_____

_____

June 7
December 7

"We have too many high-sounding words, and too few actions that correspond with them."

Abigail Adams

Actions do speak louder than words. Who do you consider to be the greatest people of action?

1. _____
   _____

2. _____
   _____

3. _____
   _____

Contact each person today and learn how he or she each became a person of action. Document what you learned.

_____
_____
_____
_____
_____

Six Months Review:

_____
_____
_____

Quotation Source Information:

_____
_____
_____

June 8
December 8

"The way to develop self confidence is to do the thing you fear."

William Jennings Bryant

Fears, whether real or imagined, keep us from reaching our full potential. List three of your biggest fears:

1. _____

   _____

2. _____

   _____

3. _____

   _____

Take the necessary steps to conquer each fear listed and brag to someone about conquering each fear.

Six Months Review:

_____

_____

_____

Quotation Source Information:

_____

_____

_____

June 9
December 9

Wealth lost—something lost;
Honor lost—much lost;
Courage lost—all lost.

German Proverb

Do you agree or disagree with this old saw? Why or why not?

_____
_____
_____
_____
_____

Six Months Review:

_____
_____
_____

Quotation Source Information:

_____
_____
_____

June 10
December 10

"Good leadership consists of showing average people how to do the work of superior people."

John D. Rockefeller

Leaders will raise the level of performance of those around them. Note people that you feel perform superior work in all that they do:

1. _____

_____

2. _____

_____

3. _____

_____

Contact each person today and learn how he or she achieved that level of superiority in his or her work. Document what you learned:

_____
_____
_____
_____
_____

Six Months Review:

_____
_____
_____

Quotation Source Information:

_____
_____
_____

June 11
December 11

"It is not the employer who pays the wages.
Employers only handle the money.
It is the customer who pays the wages."

Henry Ford

Without customers, there is no business. How have you as a customer been treated as an important part of business?

1. _____
   _____

2. _____
   _____

3. _____
   _____

4. _____
   _____

5. _____
   _____

In which ways do you place your customers as most important part of the way that you conduct your business?

1. _____
   _____

2. _____
   _____

3. _____

_____

4. _____

_____

5. _____

_____

Six Months Review:

_____

_____

_____

Quotation Source Information:

_____

_____

_____

June 12
December 12

"Leadership by example is the best example of leadership."

Richard Possett

Leadership styles run the gamut from autocracy to democracy; from benevolence to malevolence. How would you characterize your personal style of leadership?

_____
_____
_____
_____
_____

Six Months Review:

_____
_____
_____

Quotation Source Information:

_____
_____
_____

June 13
December 13

"Ideas won't keep; something must be done about them."

Alfred North Whitehead

How do you take ideas and turn them into action?

1. _____
   _____

2. _____
   _____

3. _____
   _____

Which idea will you act on today?

_____
_____
_____
_____
_____

Six Months Review:

_____
_____
_____

Quotation Source Information:

_____
_____
_____

June 14
December 14

"Everyone rises to their level of incompetence."

The Peter Principle

Unfortunately, the maxim professed by Laurence J. Peter has gravity. What specific things are you doing to ensure your ongoing personal competence?

1. _____

   _____

2. _____

   _____

3. _____

   _____

Six Months Review:

_____

_____

_____

Quotation Source Information:

_____

_____

_____

June 15
December 15

"Success is a science;
if you have the conditions, you get the result."

Oscar Wilde

Long-term success is not an accident. List ways you position your environment for success:

1. _____

   _____

2. _____

   _____

3. _____

   _____

Six Months Review:

_____

_____

_____

Quotation Source Information:

_____

_____

_____

June 16
December 16

"Give yourself something
to work toward—constantly."

Mary Kay Ash

List your three most important goals for today:

1. _____
   _____

2. _____
   _____

3. _____
   _____

Write how you are going to accomplish each goal:

_____
_____
_____
_____
_____

Do this exercise daily.

Six Months Review:

_____
_____
_____

Quotation Source Information:

_____
_____
_____

June 17
December 17

"Friendships aren't perfect, and yet they are very
precious. For me, not expecting perfection
all in one place was a great release."

Letty Cottin Pogrebin

Effective leaders don't expect perfection. Sometimes they even develop
programs and processes for mediocrity. How do you manage perfection?
Make a list for future reference. Please keep your expectations realistic.

Six Months Review:

Quotation Source Information:

June 18
December 18

"Think big. It's wonderful when it comes off."

Simeon Nkoane

When a true leader shares their vision, they are demonstrating their ability to think big. Who are some people that think bigger than you?

Name: _____
_____

Name: _____
_____

Name: _____
_____

Contact each person today and find out how they learned to think big. Document the findings:

_____
_____
_____
_____
_____

Six Months Review:

_____
_____
_____

Quotation Source Information:

_____
_____
_____

June 19
December 19

"Success is never serendipitous. Failure is never fatal.
We traverse the void through the courage
of our convictions."

Richard Possett

Some say personal courage is the first virtue of leadership. In your hierarchy of leadership qualities, where do you place courage? Why?

_____

_____

_____

_____

_____

Six Months Review:

_____

_____

_____

Quotation Source Information:

_____

_____

_____

June 20
December 20

"Have regular hours for work and play; make each day both useful and pleasant, and prove that you understand the worth of time by employing it well."

Louisa May Alcott

How do you achieve balance in your work and play time?

_____
_____
_____
_____
_____

Six Months Review:

_____
_____
_____

Quotation Source Information:

_____
_____
_____

June 21
December 21

> ## "People love others not for who they are but for how they make them feel."

Irwin Federman

Charisma was originally a religious term meaning "of the spirit" or "inspired." What tactics do you employ to encourage and excite other people?

_____
_____
_____
_____
_____

Six Months Review:

_____
_____
_____

Quotation Source Information:

_____
_____
_____

June 22
December 22

"He has the right to criticize,
who has a heart to help."

Abraham Lincoln

It is so easy to point out the faults in others. It takes leadership to build others up, even when it may be perceived that there is little to work with. Today, how can you help build others up?

1. _____
   _____

2. _____
   _____

3. _____
   _____

4. _____
   _____

5. _____
   _____

Build up others today. Record your experiences:

_____
_____
_____
_____
_____

Six Months Review:

_____

_____

_____

Quotation Source Information:

_____

_____

_____

June 23
December 23

"Aim at the sun and you may not reach it;
but your arrow will fly higher than if you had aimed
at an object on a level with yourself."

F. Hawes

Do you put any stretch in your goals? Why or why not? Today set a new objective and multiply it by 150%. Go for the goal.

_____
_____
_____
_____
_____

Six Months Review:

_____
_____
_____

Quotation Source Information:

_____
_____
_____

June 24
December 24

"Example is not the main thing
in influencing others.
It is the only thing."

Albert Schweitzer

Role models are important in life and business. Do you set good examples for other people? In your routes and routines today, consciously do three exemplary things.

1. _____

   _____

2. _____

   _____

3. _____

   _____

Six Months Review:

_____

_____

_____

Quotation Source Information:

_____

_____

_____

June 25
December 25

"The first and last task of a leader
is to keep hope alive."

John W. Gardner

Sometimes hope is easily kept, sometimes it goes onto life support.
When things got rough, list the ways that you have observed leaders
keeping hope alive:

1. _____
   _____

2. _____
   _____

3. _____
   _____

4. _____
   _____

5. _____
   _____

Six Months Review:

_____
_____
_____

Quotation Source Information:

_____
_____
_____

June 26
December 26

"Effective leaders maintain a learning posture throughout their lifetimes."

J. Robert Clinton

An incredible amount of information is available to us daily, with more information being created as you read this. How can you learn something-new everyday?

1. _____
   _____

2. _____
   _____

3. _____
   _____

4. _____
   _____

5. _____
   _____

What are the best ways you can share that knowledge daily?

1. _____
   _____

2. _____
   _____

3. _____
   _____

4. _____
   _____

5. _____
   _____

Six Months Review:

_____
_____
_____

Quotation Source Information:

_____
_____
_____

June 27
December 27

"The key to success is to get out into the store and listen to what the associates have to say."

Sam Walton

Do you do walkabouts and listen to your employees? When was the last time? What did they say?

_____

_____

_____

_____

_____

Six Months Review:

_____

_____

_____

Quotation Source Information:

_____

_____

_____

June 28
December 28

"First we form habits, then they form us."

Rob Gilbert

What is your personal list of leadership qualities?

_____
_____
_____
_____
_____

Are they your daily habits?

Six Months Review:

_____
_____
_____

Quotation Source Information:

_____
_____
_____

June 29
December 29

"For me there are simply seven attributes ascribed to a successful leader. I know because I have personally worked for three. Those attributes are: intelligence, education, knowledge, creativity, industriousness, ethics and personableness."

Richard Possett

Would you add anything to this list? Why?

_____

_____

_____

_____

_____

Would you take anything away from this list? Why?

_____

_____

_____

_____

_____

Six Months Review:

_____

_____

_____

Quotation Source Information:

_____

_____

_____

June 30
December 30

"We can have more than we've got because
we can become more than we are."

Jim Rohn

It takes much to make a good person. And that sums up a leader. In this
book we have identified numerous leadership qualities. See if you can
list all of them below.

_____

_____

_____

_____

_____

Six Months Review:

_____

_____

_____

Quotation Source Information:

_____

_____

_____

July 1
December 31

"God grant me the serenity to accept the people I cannot change, the courage to change the one I can, and the wisdom to know it's me."

Unknown

(A variation of an excerpt from "The Serenity Prayer" by Reinhold Neibuhr)

List one thing that you want to change about you.

_____
_____
_____
_____
_____

Do it!!!!!!

Six Months Review:

_____
_____
_____

Congratulations

Three cheers for making the commitment to be a more powerful person. For you see, power is that great ability to do, act, and achieve. And producing the proper level of energy to be a dynamic individual takes dedication. It is the same resolve you showed by completing and reviewing each daily assignment in this book.

John Erskine is noted for saying…"In the simplest terms, a leader is one who knows where he wants to go, and gets up and goes." Look into the mirror, this is you. For the last three hundred and sixty-six (366) days you have focused on leadership. You should feel good and proud of yourself. Each day when you woke-up you knew where you wanted to go and you went there. You did what it took to become a more learned leader. You came to see the close relationship between power and the ability to lead others. You now recognize power-driven individuals, their qualities and characteristics, and understand that powerful people are powerful leaders.

President John F. Kennedy once said…"Leadership and learning are indispensable to each other." These two attributes complement one another. For applied knowledge is the power and driving force of the effective leader. These people know; know what to do; and, know when to do it. In this book you also have learned some know-how on being a better captain of men. You have finished a milestone in your life by making a major scholarship investment into yourself. It was a good choice, bravo; well done!

If you are in the first half of this book, you have learned some of the features that are needed to be a more effective leader. If you have finished the final six months of the assignments, you have completed a year-long journey. This odyssey has sharpened your personal skills and capabilities. These traits will be needed further down the road as a power-driven person and leader of people. Charles S. Lauer is quoted as saying… "Leaders don't force people to follow; they invite them on a journey." This is good insight.

Share your new found understandings about power and leadership with others in your life. Help them to be good and show them how to get better. By helping other people to become more powerful, you make yourself a wiser and more influential individual. True leaders are great givers. By investing your time and resources into this volume of work, you have learned much and have a lot to share. Therefore, sally out into the world and give what you got and people will follow because *powerful people are powerful leaders.*

Again, congratulations on a job well done.

~ Peter Biadasz and Richard Possett

Conclusion

The conclusion is the end or the last part; the last of a chain of events. But, when you think about it, the end of this book is really a starting. You have just finished the footwork, and now the bout actually begins. It is your commencement where you start putting to work your new learned leadership skills. As Harold Geneen sagely said, "Leadership cannot really be taught. It can only be learned." The implication here is that leadership is an applied craft honed through involvement and participation. Therefore, you must take your new found artistry into the real world and put it to good use. Realizing the utility of your efforts will make all of your life-work more meaningful, productive, and powerful.

According to Peter Drucker… "Leadership is lifting a person's vision to higher sights, the raising of a person's performance to a higher standard, the building of a personality beyond its normal limitations." Mr. Drucker's statement is a high powered charge or summons. Still, the command is doable because of all the mental effort you have exerted to make yourself a more powerful leader of people. In the first half of the book, you have absorbed the quotations and educated yourself about the author or the quote source. You have worked through the exercises. Now, you are fully prepared due to the fact that you have thoughtfully and thoroughly completed each daily lesson.

In the second six months of the assignments, you have carefully reviewed, reevaluated, and reapplied your work. You have made the necessary and appropriate adjustments to the output. During this period of time, you have practiced what you have learned. All of these concluded tasks have made you a better leader and thus, a more powerful person.

You did it on your own. You did it in private. Now, fully infuse this power into your daily life. Take it public. Release the new found power of leadership into your personal and professional activities with energy and force.

You already know that powerful people are powerful leaders. You read about them in books, magazines, and newspapers. Everyday, you see them on television, learn about them on the internet, and hear them on the radio. So, if you have carefully read this book and diligently completed the exercises, then you have made the choice to be more powerful. And, success and power are nurtured by the same essential quality, effective leadership. Now, go forth and lead knowing you have the knowledge and the power for success because *powerful people are powerful leaders.*

About The Authors

Peter Biadasz (pronounced *bee-ahd-ish*) has been in numerous leadership positions in many groups and organizations since junior high school. As a leader Peter not only shares his vision for each organization and the office that he holds, but carefully leads the members to fulfill the vision in a manner that creates win/win scenarios that are in the best interest of the organization. Having taught leadership skills numerous times, Peter has been known to utilize his professional trumpet talent to liven up speaking engagements.

Peter is a graduate of Florida State University. His passion for and expertise in the area of leadership has aided many over the years. Leadership and the skills required to become a great leader are essential in reaching the next level of success. Experience has shown that the people and groups working with Peter have an increase in the quality of leadership skills. Furthermore, an excitement for the topics at hand, as never before seen, emerges as those involved transform into distinguished and mature leaders.

The father of an incredible son and precious daughter, Peter is also the author of *MORE LEADS: The Complete Handbook for TIPS Groups, Leads Groups, and Networking Groups* and co-author of the Power Series, of which this book is a part. Please visit with Peter at www.getmoreleads.net or www.bepowerful.net.

Richard Possett is a forty-five year experienced entrepreneur and seasoned executive from the international financial and insurance services industries. As a successful businessman, Richard has spent decades leading people into new endeavors and to greater heights of performance. Throughout a long and industrious career, his guiding motto has been and continues to be: "The best example of leadership is leadership by example."

Richard was born and raised in Grand Rapids, Michigan. He lived and worked for five years in Los Angeles, California, before moving to Mid-America where he and his family have resided for the last eighteen years.

Richard graduated from Western Michigan University with a BBA degree earning a major in accountancy. He is a CPA, retired executive, small business owner, accredited mortgage loan originator, financialist and past SEC-registered securities representative and licensed insurance agent.

Richard is a former international rugby player. He served in the United States Army during the Vietnam War. He has been married to his best friend and partner for more than forty-two (42) wonderful years. The couple has three awesome adult children; three beautiful young grand-children and a great son-in-law. Richard's interests are reading, writing and walking with his wife and their two golden retrievers, Jordie and Doolie.

Richard is an award winning author. For a complete catalogue of his literary works, visit www.bepossettive.com. To personally contact the author, please feel free to email him at richard@bepossitive.com. He would love to hear from everyone-everywhere.

Index Of Individuals Quoted

Index Of Topics Quoted

Note: Many quotes may fit into more than one category.

A Chuncated Approach

'Power~Series'

Ben Franklin was a brilliant gentleman and a great moral exemplar. Furthermore, he possessed a myriad of supremely admirable skills and talents. One of Franklin's many gifts was the extraordinary ability to see potential and then realize it. An area in which this aptitude was truly manifested was in the development of Franklin's moral excellence. Early on in life he had actualized his very own *chuncated* training regimen for goodness called the thirteen virtues. Franklin wrote out a list of these ideals and had them printed in a table made up of seven columns (one for each day of the week) and thirteen rows (one for each virtue). He then placed a black spot in the appropriate square each time he failed to live that day in agreement with a particular attribute. At first, Franklin concentrated on only one quality each week, hoping to keep its row clear of spots while paying no special attention to the other characteristics. Over thirteen weeks, he worked through the whole matrix. Then he repeated the process, finding that with repetition the table got less and less spotty. Franklin wrote in his autobiography that, though he fell short of perfection: "I was, by the endeavor, a better and happier man than I otherwise should have been if I had not attempted it." From this approach, Franklin *chuncated* himself to moral excellence one day at a time. For a full explanation of the virtues, please go to www.school-for-champions.com or simply Google the internet.

As you can see, *chuncated* learning has been around at least, if not longer, since the beginning of the republic. It is a time-tested methodology of erudition. It is a highly effective way of developing character and

219

personality, acquiring information, and applying knowledge. We call this technique the Chuncated Learning System, or "CLS." CLS is a compelling way of cultivating positive growth and change in both your personal and professional lives. For this reason, chuncated learning is the chosen method that is used in the 'Power~Series' books. CLS is a highly cogent manner for changing personality style gradually by mastering and applying facts and ideas incrementally.

A big part of CLS is the small. This is because the process takes a large body of work and breaks it down into little enjoyable pieces. CLS is effective because it teaches a big concept in small daily bite sizes of knowledge. It is a wise-way we term "chunking." The approach takes a huge hunk of education and breaks it down into wee nuggets for easier learning. It is very much like baby steps. That is, scholarship in tiny short strides.

In each 'Power~Series' book, there are exercises to be completed, reviewed, and revised over a period of one year. These tasks are assigned as home school, to be done daily in a fun, fast, and easy fashion. Empirically, we have come to know that the earthborn learn best from consistent daily study and practice. This mode easily reframes and reinforces the specific subject matter. So then, over many days and weeks, new knowledge is accumulated and a new awareness of oneself emerges, shaping a powerfully enhanced neo-personality style.

With each simple assignment thoroughly and thoughtfully completed, the student of a 'Power~Series' book receives a modicum of wisdom in the form of a small reward, a little flash of accomplishment. It is an ecstatic titillation of self-admiration; a euphoric sense of self-confidence emboldened by achievement. This sensation is the wonderfully good feeling of a personal job well done. And each shot of "feel-good" is like a hulking reward reinforcing a newly learned chunked concept. By gradually shaping, hunk-by-chunk, your thoughts and actions, CLS strongly influences an improved personality style having the power of presence and poise. It hones your latent power-driven traits and talents for a new and improved powerfully you.

Furthermore, CLS was adopted for the 'Power~Series' books because of its simple and straightforward approach to learning. In the hurly-burly of modern society, it is often difficult, as an adult, to continue one's education and self development. The strictures of home, work, and family responsibilities can frequently retard your personal growth and the capability to improve the self. CLS, with its "chunking" process, helps to materially mitigate the constraints of time. By simply setting aside a very small part of your busy day and focusing on learning in bite sizes, you can grow more powerful with your newly applied knowledge, one day at a time.

The 'Power Series' Books

The 'Power Series' books mean what they say and say what they mean. They are powerful and contain the dynamism to make you a power-driven person. The books are about the reader learning how to effectively acquire and utilize productive power in all facets of their life; personal and professional; at home, work, and play. The books are not concerned with dominion, authority, and control. These books are about health, wealth, and happiness. The 'Power Series' books provide the principles and practices that can produce a lifestyle full wellness and success.

There are many-many elements that make a power person. Such essentials as relationships, leadership, networking, teaching, listening, learning, spirituality, character, and health, make a short and incomplete list. The material and information in the power-books speak to what it takes to be powerful in living life. The aforementioned areas are part and parcel of what it takes to be a powerful person. The syllabus could go on ad infinitum. Currently, 'Power Series' book titles include:

Powerful People Have Powerful Character
Powerful People Overcome Powerful Failures
Powerful People Play Powerful Golf
Powerful People Have Powerful Health
Powerful People Are Powerful I.T. Professionals
Powerful People Are Powerful Learners
Powerful People Are Powerful Listeners
Powerful People Have Powerful Meekness
Powerful People Have Powerful Money
Powerful People Are Powerful Networkers
Powerful People Are Powerful Performers
Powerful People Have Powerful Personalities
Powerful People Have Powerful Relationships
Powerful People Are Powerful Risk Managers
Powerful People Are Powerful Teachers
More Power Titles to Be Released Next Year

To learn more about the 'Power Series' as well as to order additional books, please visit www.bepowerful.net. The 'Power Series' books are the production of Peter Biadasz and Richard Possett. You can learn more about the producers in the "About the Authors" section of the book you are now holding in your hands.

978-0-595-41218-1
0-595-41218-1

www.ingramcontent.com/pod-product-compliance
Lightning Source LLC
Chambersburg PA
CBHW020741180526

45163CB00001B/302